How To Use

YOUR TWELVE GIFTS FROM GOD

How to Use
YOUR
TWELVE
GIFTS
FROM
GOD

William A. Warch

DeVorss & Company

P.O. Box 550
Marina del Rey, California 90294

ISBN: 0-87516-530-3

Library of Congress
Catalog Card Number: 76-41588

Third paperback printing, 1989
published by DeVorss & Company

Cover Photo by Ray Highfill

Printed in the United States of America

Contents

To Reverend David and Reverend Marge Peterson

INTRODUCTION

You have opened this book and are reading the words on this page as part of God's divine plan for your spiritual unfoldment. You have a magnificent purpose on this planet earth! Mankind is the only entity on earth that can think in abstracts. Therefore, the destiny of the earth is in the consciousness of mankind. The greatest thing you can do is to dedicate yourself to the development of your consciousness.

You have within your consciousness twelve wonderful "Gifts" from God. Your awareness of these gifts will help you in your spiritual development. Balancing these gifts in every daily experience will lead to inner peace and perfect harmony both within yourself and with the world.

Admittedly you may not know how God works, but you do know that he does. It is through understanding your gifts as God-given tools that you may begin to apply the correct tool for the correct resolution. Rather than trying to figure out how Spirit works, just become receptive to the divine activity taking place within you now. When you still yourself toward a specific gift, your consciousness is altered, and you will actually start developing in that area. This is the balancing process in developing your Spiritual awareness.

As you read about a particular gift it refreshes your mind to your inner abilities, your divine powers. When you still yourself toward a particular gift

1

it is activated in your consciousness and it will transform you! Now remember, your inner transformation causes outer conditions to change also. This is an exciting step in God's divine unfoldment for you. You will learn to call upon a gift by becoming silent, still, and receptive to the Spiritual activity of that gift within you. As you still yourself toward a gift, you may or may not feel a physical sensation. Either way, simply know that an inner transformation is taking place, that you are being raised to the consciousness of your spiritual self.

Each gift in this book is presented first with some basic statements for you to read and learn. Absorb them into your consciousness before proceeding. A Preview about each gift will briefly outline the basic points that will be covered in the content. The content is followed by specific Scriptures that deal with each gift from the *Authorized King James Version* of the *Holy Bible*.

Be sure to read over the questions at the end of each section and write down or think out each answer. This will help you to more thoroughly absorb each gift into your conscious awareness. Then repeat each Denial and Affirmation slowly, at least three times. You will find that as challenges arise during each day, your mind seeks out the gift that will help you keep in balance. As you apply these gifts, and balance your consciousness, you will find yourself moving through each challenge with ease.

You will probably read and re-read this book several times until the day comes when you have locked the information deep within your heart. You will find yourself at a point where you can give your book away to someone else who needs it more than yourself; for on that day you will simply still yourself in the face of any challenge, call on your gifts, and move through your challenge with an inner peace and an outward glow.

Without the inspiration from the writings by Charles Fillmore in, *"Twelve Powers of Man"*, and Ed Rabel's excellent cassette series under the same title, this book would not have been possible. The *"Science of Mind"* textbook by Ernest Holmes offered additional concepts that were invaluable. My highest gratitude and respect to these inspired men. I recommend these books and the cassette series to all Truth Students who wish to increase their knowledge of their "Twelve Gifts From God".✳

✳Charles Fillmore and Ed Rabel's works may be obtained from Unity Village, Missouri.
Ernest Holmes books are available in most Religeous Science bookstores.

FAITH

FAITH   is my ability to say "Yes" to God and Good.

FAITH   draws my good from the invisible to the visible.

5

PREVIEW

1. God is invisible.

2. FAITH is your ability to say "Yes" to God.

3. FAITH is your ability to draw your good from the invisible to the visible.

4. FAITH and belief are not the same.

5. You develop your awareness of FAITH by exercising it.

In order to understand the purpose and function of your wonderful gift of Faith you must consider the nature of God. First, God is all your good, the source of everything you need spiritually and materially. But this source is invisible. And in the invisible it remains as potential, not necessarily a part of your living experience. Naturally, you want to experience your good. You want to have your needs met. So you need the ability to draw out from the invisible all your good. You want to develop the ability to receive the countless blessings that rest as potential in God, the invisible Source.

How do you actively involve yourself in the process of drawing your good from God? By using Faith! Faith is your affirmative power. It is your ability to say "Yes" to God and to your good. Simply acknowledging your needs doesn't mean that your needs will be met. You must also acknowledge that which you need and say "Yes" to it. Say "Yes" to God and your good and move it into your living experience. Saying "Yes" to perfect transportation is a far cry from acknowledging a broken down car. Complaining and being angry drains that very energy that could be directed toward drawing your good from your invisible Source. Faith is a tool with which to build a higher consciousness.

Let's take a look at your level of consciousness. Your level of consciousness is supported by your subconscious. That which you believe in, love, fear, or hate, at the subconscious level, determines your conscious perception of reality. It determines your viewpoints and attitudes. There are many wonderful positive attitudes you have built into your subconscious by saying "Yes" to them. If you have a prosperity consciousness you have said "Yes" so often to prosperity that you have built it into your subconscious. Perhaps your parents trained you to think positive, or your surroundings exemplified prosperity. In some manner you accepted into your consciousness prosperity so thoroughly that it became programmed into your subconscious so that you do not think about it anymore. In other words, if it is programmed into your subconscious to where you don't have to think about it to receive it, you have a prosperity consciousness. You know prosperity. You are prosperity. You live it without thinking about it. You have a "Yes" attitude toward it and are constantly drawing it to you from God. How do you draw your good from the invisible to the visible? By saying "Yes" to God and your good.

You can see that Faith is a consciousness building faculty in that you can use it to lift yourself from one limited level by saying "Yes" to a greater level. If you want to lift yourself to a greater awareness of health, for example, and experience it in your life, you must develop an attitude of health that becomes a very part of your knowing. Someone might say, "Cure me and then I will believe". It is exactly the reverse. That is "seeing is believing". Actually, you must believe before you can be cured. You have never been cured by a doctor unless you thought you could be. The medicine arrested the disease but the healing power was due to your attitude of health. Without an attitude of health in the consciousness there would be no healing. It is exciting to realize that a negative consciousness can be transformed by using the power of Faith. If you realize there is a negative attitude in your consciousness, one that is drawing unhappiness into your living experience, let it be replaced by your use of Faith.

At this point I would like to clarify some misconceptions about Faith. You have heard people say, "I just don't have faith anymore". This statement reveals that they do not understand the nature and purpose of Faith. Faith is not something you have or have not. No one has more Faith than anyone else. Faith is a God given quality, one of the main twelve, that makes up your spiritual nature. You do not have Faith; you are Faith. You have no choice in the matter. It is one of the characteristics you have that is likened to God. God is Faith and you are Faith. God is the power that brings good from the invisible to the visible and you have the power in you, God in you, to bring forth your good from invisible Divine energy. So Faith is not something you have or have not. It is your God given ability to draw your good from the invisible to the visible.

Now we come to an important part of Faith and that is Belief. There is a difference between belief and

Faith. You can believe anything. You can believe in sickness or health, wealth or poverty, intelligence or ignorance. That belief will draw to you whatever you believe in. But Faith does not draw negatives. Belief can be involved in fear as well as security. Faith in God is drawing your security and a sense of well being to you. So if you find yourself drawing something harmful to yourself you have belief in it, but you don't have Faith in it. The gift of Faith in you relates only to God and your good.

You may wonder what the purpose of belief is. Faith without belief is like having a fortune and forgetting where you put it. Everyone has the gift of Faith but not everyone has an active Faith. Everyone has the ability to draw his good from the invisible but not everyone does it. Belief is the activator of Faith. When you believe your good can be drawn to you then your Faith moves it into expression. This is why affirmations may need to be repeated many times until you believe them. When your subconscious accepts your affirmation, you as a spiritual being give God permission to move through you as a fulfillment. You can see how important it is to really believe in God. Even though you have the gift of faith it cannot be exercised until you believe in God and good. So Faith without belief lies dormant. Belief without Faith in God can draw anything to you, good or bad.

This answers the question, "Why are some of my prayers not answered?" Because you prayed for something that was not right for you. Your gift of Faith will not bring something into your life that is not right for you. Belief will but Faith won't. Whenever you completely hand it over to God you will have only good results.

Let's be specific about how to exercise Faith. Let's say you want to fly to Hawaii but you havn't the money for air fare. If you believe in God you know that all things are possible. But at the same time, not all things are right for you. So you rely on Faith knowing that God will provide the air fare if it is right for you to go. You find some quiet place to meditate. You affirm, "There is nothing preventing me from going to Hawaii; the money is flowing to me now." Then you release all concerns and still yourself toward Divine Faith. You give silent time for God to alter your consciousness, removing any doubts. The instant you truly accept it in your consciousness the way clears for you to go. Ideas come or a letter arrives. If you find that it does not work out that you go to Hawaii, your prayer is still answered. It wasn't right for you to go at this time. But your desire led you another step of the way to spiritual awareness. When you release all outcomes to the Wisdom of God the results are spiritual growth. Remember, Faith draws only your good. You could cling to the idea of going to Hawaii and force the issue by overborrowing or manipulating a friend, but that will not exercise Faith. That is personal will power.

What do you desire to bring to your life? Pray knowing and believing that it is yours, then turn it over to God, release it. Trust God that the results of your prayer will be only for good. Make your decisions based on the inner instructions you receive and be obedient in your listening. Then, above all, still yourself toward your divine gift of Faith, knowing that it is being exercised for your good. Take time every day to say "Yes" to your hearts' desires. The more

10

you accept them as possibilities the more you are adjusting within to accepting them. Exercise your Faith. There is no need to leave your good as dormant potential. Exercise your Faith. Bring God and good into your living human and spiritual experience.

SCRIPTURE

"According to thy Faith be it unto you." (Mat. 9:29)
"Lord, I believe; help thou my unbelief." (Mk. 9:24)
"Blessed are they that have not seen, and yet have believed." (Jn. 29:29)
"Now Faith is the substance of things hoped for, the evidence of things not seen." (He. 11:1)

QUESTIONS

1. How do you actively use faith?
2. Is it important to know what you want when using faith?
3. What is the relationship between your subconscious and your consciousness?
4. How does Faith effect consciousness building?
5. Can you have Faith in illness?
6. Can you have less Faith than someone else?
7. What is meant by developing Faith?
8. What is the difference between Faith and belief?
9. What is the purpose of Faith?

10. What is the purpose of belief?
11. Why are some prayers not answered?
12. How would you go about drawing some specific good into your life?

DENIAL

Doubt and fear of the unknown have no place in my mind or heart.

AFFIRMATION

From God, through me, good pours forth into the world as perfect manifestation.

STRENGTH

STRENGTH is my ability to be still.

STRENGTH allows me to stick with divine ideas.

STRENGTH is my patience, tolerance, steadfastness,
and balance.

PREVIEW

1. STRENGTH is stillness.

2. STRENGTH has four spiritual aspects: patience, tolerance, steadfastness, and balance.

3. STRENGTH is derived from the balance between your thinking and feeling.

4. There are two uses of STRENGTH: spiritual and physical

There are many misconceptions about strength that have caused you to squander your energies. You have heard the phrase, "Don't just stand there, do something". It seems that strength has been associated with physical exertion, force, and pressure. But how many times have you found all your pushing around to be a waste of time? Reacting to a situation by pushing back is not the answer; it is not really a sign of strength. A more popular phrase has been coined, "Don't just do something, stand there!" This is because we are coming to realize that activity in itself is not strength. Rather than being a noisy, exerting attribute, strength is stillness. You find your strength in the stillness and the silence of your being. This is how you find your confidence and security: by being still.

True strength gives you a greater power than the ability to move "things" about. One of the wonderful ways strength manifests itself in your consciousness is in the form of patience. Patience is calm, uncomplaining endurance. It is persistent courage. Whenever you need to be courageous in a situation, all you need to do is become still. It is a deliberate spiritual step when you still yourself toward something spiritual. Still yourself toward strength, and a quiet courage comes forth through your consciousness as patience. If you do not draw upon your source of patience you become irritable and tense and have no other choice than to react in anger and impatience. You always have the choice of waiting upon your Lord rather than becoming frustrated and embittered. Draw upon strength as patience.

Another wonderful way in which spiritual strength manifests itself through your consciousness is in the form of tolerance. Tolerance is your ability to be fair to those with whom you do not agree. This gives you freedom from bigotry. It is your ability to allow deviation from conformity, keeping you open and flexible. Many times you have met someone who has believed differently from you or who lives a life style that seems extraordinary. But you must realize that this person is at his level of consciousness and needs the freedom to experience life through his own choices. If it is incompatible with your ways and you sense a strain due to difference, you may draw upon divine strength and have it manifest in your consciousness as tolerance. This frees both of you from struggling with your differences. It allows you calmness and serenity while acknowledging your individuality.

All strength originates in Spirit and manifests in many wonderful ways through your consciousness. Steadfastness is a third way in which you benefit by placing God at the head of your life. It is your ability to stay fixed in a direction and unwavering in spite of all appearances. It keeps you firm in purpose. It is your ability to be firmly established in Faith rather than fickle and "on again, off again". Steadfastness is a great compliment to Faith because it allows you to "stick with it," so to speak. Many people begin developing their awareness of Faith but soon drop the whole thing at the first great challenge. Strength in the form of steadfastness is unwavering. True spiritual strength sees that your choices result in upward movements rather than in random up and down experiences. Depression and discouragement are overcome by drawing upon strength as the energy of God. They are but mere temporary experiences when you still yourself to your source of strength.

Balance is the fourth result of spiritual strength. It is mental stability in the face of variants. You have the ability to right yourself when outer pressures are exerted upon you. You do this by drawing upon strength, recognizing it as the true source of power. The instant that you feel that an outer agent has power over you, you can be pushed off center. Stilling yourself toward Divine Strength results in a habit of calm behavior, dissolving any power anyone may hold over you. Balancing yourself allows you to return to your original position, and we all know that our original position is being one with God. So, whenever you find yourself malfunctioning, allowing yourself to be pushed into a consciousness of resentment and imbalance, still yourself toward strength and draw it into your consciousness. This returns you to the presence of God and a feeling of security and well-being.

The subject of balance leads us to a very important

16

area in regards to consciousness development. You have a thinking nature and you have a feeling nature. Your greatest key to spiritual strength is through finding a balance between the two. In Bible symbolism, the male characters represent your thinking nature and the female characters represent your feeling nature. God is both male and female, or thinking and feeling. In their most highly developed state they are recognized as Divine Wisdom and Infinite Love. Everything that is recorded and accepted by your consciousness is filtered and interpreted by your thinking and feeling natures. Facts and events have their impact on you according to what you think about them and how you feel about them. The ideal is when you use wisdom and love in dealing with outer conditions and people. But sometimes negative thinking can throw you out of balance. If negative thinking predominates your mind, you will find yourself spiritually depleted and struggling against a sense of weakness. You will lack patience, tolerance, steadfastness, and balance. It is vital that you restore the balance between your thinking and feeling as quickly as possible.

You must use your feeling nature to uplift your thinking when you have been overcome by negative vibrations. Strive for a sense of well-being and return to the source of your being. Allow Divine Love to permeate your consciousness and release your negative throughts, realizing that they are not the Truth. They are based on mere facts which are alterable through the Love of God.

On the other hand, if you are out of balance due to negative emotions, you must use positive thinking to correct this state. Feeling despair and discouragement can be corrected through positively affirming the truth. By using your word of truth based upon divine principles, you can uplift your feeling nature to a state of love and serenity. In Bible symbolism, adultery is associating your feeling nature with negative thinking or associating your thinking nature with negative feelings. Both states of consciousness are draining and result in spiritual weakness and physical ineffectiveness. When you are feeling good and thinking right, you are experiencing great strength in your consciousness. Strength comes out of balance. The perfect marriage is the divine combination of love and wisdom in your consciousness. This is the balance to seek in your spiritual development.

Why do you really need strength? You need it as a tool in consciousness development. And, being human, you utilize strength for your human, as well as spiritual needs. In the worldly situation, you spend strength to guard posessions and to maintain self-preservation. In the spiritual sense, you spend strength for patience, tolerance, steadfastness, and balance. Both areas are legitimate areas in which to utilize your spiritual gift of strength, but you can see that strength has to cover a lot of territory. Strength must be replenished regularly for an adequate duration of time. Turning to the silence and stillness of your Source is a must to maintain the ability to stay in balance. Should you deplete your supply of spiritual energy, there comes a sense of separateness from God. Then you will resort to sheer personal will power. At this point, your thoughts and feelings are governed by outer conditions and appearances. You can survive in this state of consciousness, but you will not develop spiritually. Regularly, still yourself toward Divine Strength so you can always sense your oneness with God and be patient, tolerant, steadfast, and in balance.

SCRIPTURE

"The Lord is the strength of my life." (Ps. 27:1)
"Cast thy burden upon the Lord, and He shall sustain thee." (Ps. 55:22)
"Their strength is to sit still." (Is. 39:7)

QUESTIONS

1. Is influencing people a sign of strength?
2. How would you define patience?
3. How would you define tolerance?
4. How would you define steadfastness?
5. How would you define balance?
6. Are the five senses the avenues through which your consciousness is effected?
7. Give an instance of being out of balance in your thinking.
8. Give an instance of being out of balance in your feeling.
9. Is strength to be utilized for spiritual growth?
10. How does strength relate to faith?
11. Is it important to know the difference between Faith and Strength?

DENIAL

I deny any sense of weakness or despair.

AFFIRMATION

Divine Strength surges through me now as energy, encouragement, and patience.

JUDGEMENT

JUDGEMENT   *is my ability to discern, evaluate, and make decisions.*

JUDGEMENT   *allows Divine Wisdom to flow through me.*

PREVIEW

1. JUDGEMENT has two functions: drawing upon Spirit for guidance, and conclusion making.

2. In listening for guidance, JUDGEMENT is used in three ways: discerning, evaluating, and decision making.

3. Proper exercising of JUDGEMENT reveals that Divine Wisdom and your intuition are the same.

4. Regret is a crippler.

How exciting it is to learn about yet another of the spiritual gifts that God has implanted in you as a tool for spiritual development. The two purposes of your judgement faculty are, one, the drawing upon Spirit for guidance and, two, the ability to come to conclusions. In common terms, we would call them "using good judgement" and "making judgements". Let us deal with the latter purpose, that of making judgements, and consider its importance in consciousness building.

God is often referred to as Divine Mind. In Divine Mind, there are no such things as capacities, stages, boundaries, or scope. God is all that is, limitless and all intelligence. Note I did not say intelligent, rather I said intelligence. As a human being, you are unable to comprehend all that is. You can comprehend only so much at a time until you are ready for more. Often, you need to rest on a subject until you incorporate it into your consciousness. At each resting point you need to conclude on the information, deciding what you think and how you feel about it. In other words, you come to many conclusions as you develop and grow. If you are extremely open, you are willing to release old conclusions in order to conclude upon greater concepts and insights. So, you are making judgements constantly as you grow, step by step, moving from one conclusion to another. The wonderful thing about making judgements is that they become a reality for you. Imagine you can judge everything wonderful and good, and that is the world you will live in, wonderful and good. You can judge things to be ugly and distasteful, and these conclusions will prove you absolutely right. Ugly and distasteful things will manifest in your life.

You need to be aware of a special quality about your judgement making. It has a rapidfire action. Whereas Faith and Strength have a duration involved in their development, making judgements is instantaneous in its effect on your consciousness. Jesus warns us of this special nature of judgement in the seventh chapter of the book of Matthew, "Judge not, that ye be not judged: and with what measure ye mete, it shall be measured to you again". So, whatever you judge, in reality you are judging yourself. The warning is well taken. Don't be too quick to judge someone negatively, because you are judging yourself. Their negative behavior has only released a bad feeling that you had about yourself all along. Your judgement faculty has detected this negativity and can bless you if you honestly admit that your emotions were stirred through seeing yourself in that person. If, however, you must defend yourself against the truth, you will declare the other person bad, denying that you are anything like that. Soon after, you will experience negative emotions as your consciousness tries to digest this sad conclusion.

But your judgements and conclusion making are assisting you in both Faith and Strength. As you grow in these areas, you are constantly coming to conclusions as to how strong and wonderful you are in the image and likeness of God. With each conclusion, you make ready for new revelation and deeper insights. Good judgement making assists you in accepting the Invisible as your Source and Strength.

The other purpose of your incredible gift of Judgement is that of drawing upon Spirit for guidance. Consciousness building comes through choice making, and you do not grow spiritually until your choices are based on spiritual guidance. Spiritual guidance is constantly offered you from within, and when you deal with outer things based upon this inner instruction, it is called using good judgement.

In dealing with outer things and conditions spiritually, there are three stages you go through very quickly. These are discernment, evaluation, and decision making. Discernment allows you to seperate the various factors involved. Situations in life can be very complex and overwhelming and your judgement faculty will give you the ability to discern the difference among things. This sorting of facts prevents you from being emotionally swayed by appeal of the senses.

Evaluation is the next step in using good judgement. Now that your discernment has separated the facts, you can evaluate them. It is important to give proper value to the various aspects of a situation, or else emotion will rule. Emotion and appeal are not the same thing as good judgement in themselves. Good judgement is when you see things in perspective and can make decisions based upon the priorities of your consciousness development. For example, a person may want to buy a particular new house. The buying of a new house is a complicated endeavor with persuasion and emotional appeal often involved. When something gets too complicated, you don't know which way to turn, which choice to make. This is the point where you must still yourself to your divine gift of Judgement. The moment you do, things begin to clear up to where you can evaluate the various factors such as price, size, location, nearby parks, and so on. Then you can make a choice based upon good judgement, so that you can come to a decision. Once you decide what is right for you or what is wrong for you, you can make choices. And remember, consciousness building comes through choice making. If you are not making choices based upon spiritual guidance, you are probably in turmoil over indecision and emotional confusion.

Now, let us really look at the source of your gift of Judgement. Divine mind is all intelligence and when this intelligence affects the world, it comes through mankind as Judgement. Here is a very important point. The exercising of Judgement is a thinking process, but drawing upon Judgement is a feeling process. Your message from God will come through your feeling nature as a "yes" feeling or a "no" feeling. This positive or negative feeling that comes from within is called intuition. Your intuition will never fail you if you still yourself to Divine

Judgement and allow the discerning, evaluating, and decision-making processes to begin. If you stay calm and centered through the process, ideas will form in your mind, and events will come into your life that will show you just how to go about carrying out your instructions. Hence, you exercise excellent judgement even though a situation might be very complex. Remember, in stilling yourself toward Divine Judgement, don't try to figure out solutions for yourself. Release the situation into the hands of your Father and allow the right feeling to take over your consciousness. This is the Christ as Judgement transforming you from within. Your intuition will register as a feeling of direction for you, revealing that which is right or wrong for you. All results will reveal that you are a channel which allows Divine Wisdom to flow through. Divine Wisdom is God in his vastness flowing through as intuition. Your ability to draw upon infinite Divine Wisdom is your gift of Judgement.

As of yet, you do not exercise perfect Judgement, but you are in the process of learning how. It is perfectly natural to make mistakes along the way. But mistake making is an area where you have to be careful about mixing the use of Judgement and judgement making with negative emotions. It is damaging to judge yourself over using poor judgement. This is called regret. As you know, regret is a feeling of loss and sorrow and can result in self-condemnation and punishment. You must remember that your intuition is a guidance system, a system that gives you direction as to which way to go. It does not give you concrete black-and-white answers. It is vital that you become involved in the process of following this guidance, learning to turn left and then right. No turn or choice is actually a mistake. It is a sign to change direction in order to remain on course. If you declare one of your adjustments as a regretful mistake, you stop growing. Feeling sorry and lamenting stops your growth. Just as Lot's wife sorrowfully looked back at her past and became a pillar of salt, you too will become immobilized with regret. It is important to release so-called mistakes and name them valuable experiences. Regret is a crippler to consciousness development. Remember, a good, honest mistake is still a forward motion.

It takes Faith to trust your Judgement. It also takes Strength to stick with good Judgement when appearances would distract you. It is important to still yourself toward your Christ self daily, allowing Faith, Strength, and good Judgement to fill you to overflowing. Otherwise, you are not equipped to meet challenges that will ask you to grow and stretch. Decide every day to communicate with God. That is good Judgement.

SCRIPTURES

"*Execute judgement in the morning.*" (Je. 21:12)
"*Judge not, that ye be not judged.*" (Mat. 7:1)
"*Out of thine own mouth will I judge thee.*" (Lu. 19:22)
"*Judge not according to appearances, but judge righteous judgement.*" (Jn. 7:24)
"*Who art thou that judgest another man's servent? To his own master he standeth or falleth.*" (Ro. 14:4)

QUESTIONS

1. What are the two functions of your gifts of Judgement?
2. Is God intelligent?
3. Is it wrong to make any judgements?
4. How do conclusions relate to spiritual development?
5. Do your judgements affect your enviornment?
6. How does your judgement of others relate to you?
7. What is discernment?
8. What is evaluation?
9. What is decision making?
10. What is choice making?
11. What is the relationship between Divine Wisdom, intuition, and judgement?
12. What effect does regret have on the function of Judgement?
13. What is the purpose of a mistake?

DENIAL

I release any pressure of decision making.

AFFIRMATION

God as Divine Judgement is bringing to light my perfect direction.

LOVE

LOVE is my ability to know oneness with all.

LOVE is my ability to desire that only good come to all.

LOVE harmonizes.

29

PREVIEW

1. LOVE is not an emotion.

2. LOVE is the ability to know oneness with all.

3. LOVE is the ability to desire that only good comes to all.

4. Gravity is a high form of LOVE.

5. LOVE is the great harmonizer.

The sum total of all twelve of your spiritual gifts equals the Christ. As you have probably come to realize by now, developing a balance in the awareness of these twelve is your mission for Christ awareness. The word "balance"is a key to spiritual sensitivity and will appear time and again in the study of your twelve gifts from God.

A very important balance that must be established in your consciousness is between your thinking nature and your feeling nature. In Bible symbology, your masculine characteristics (male characters) fall under the category of your thinking nature, while your feminine characteristics (female characters) fall under your feeling nature. There are times, however, when a highly-evolved male character will represent a feminine feeling quality and vice versa. Love is expressed in your consciousness through your feeling nature and is an important spiritual tool in developing and balancing your feeling nature with your thinking nature. Lack of balance results in intellectualism or emotionalism. Neither of these extremes result in Christ awareness, so you can see how important the balance between the two is.

Love is a spiritual gift, and it may surprise you to know that it is not an emotion. It is often confused with emotion because it is expressed through the feeling nature, just as emotion is. But Love is a spiritual quality which is drawn upon to settle emotion and to balance the feeling nature. More often than not, Love is surrounded by emotion to the point where we have confused it with emotion. Therefore, there is the mistaken idea that love includes turbulence and stress. This is untrue. Emotion can include turbulence and stress and can accompany Love, but it is not actually the divine gift of Love itself.

You may ask, "How can I tell whether or not I am experiencing genuine love toward a person or emotion?" There is one way you can always tell. Ask yourself whether or not you have any conditions on your love toward this person. Must they have a certain manner for you to love them? Must they love you in return to receive your love? Do you require that they believe a certain way for you to love them? In other words, if you have conditions on your love toward a person, it is not love. It is emotionalism. Emotionalism results in what could be called "conditional love", and this is merely the seeking to have ones own needs met. If your love is based primarily on having your own needs met, it is not the Love of God. It is your personal love based upon emotional needs. And it is important to emphasize at this point that we all have emotional needs. It is not wrong to seek fulfillment of these needs from the personal love of another. Just don't confuse it with Divine Love, the spiritual gift that God has implanted within you.

If true love is not to satisfy personal emotional needs, then what is its purpose? One of its purposes is that of equipping you with the ability to know your oneness with all. In reality, that which supports the universe, a tree, yourself, and other people, is God. Everything and everybody comes from God. Everything and everybody is God expressed into visibility. We are all one. Being able to recognize this oneness is Love, because it is the ability to recognize God. If you think about it, the only way you can see God is through these various forms of expression such as trees, mountains, animals, and people. You have a greater ability than just the physical mental process of seeing with the eyes. You can recognize your oneness with all your heart as well. Through your thinking nature you can recognize outer things. But is is only through your feeling nature that you can recognize the great common denominator of all that is. Love is your ability to know your oneness with all. It transcends outer differences to join you with all in a sense of oneness.

Love is your ability to desire that only good come to all. In a worldly consciousness of limitation, it is easy to believe that there is only so much good to go around. There is the belief that there is only so much love, so much housing, so much food, so much money. With this consciousness comes the feeling that, "I had better get mine, or someone else will get my share". It is a consciousness of amounts and portions and possessions. Unfortunately, conclusions are drawn that lead you to hoping that someone else comes to a disadvantage so that you can take advantage. It's the old game of one-upmanship. True love is unlimited and seeks only that good comes to all.

Jealousy is the fear that another person will get more love than you. Some say that they love another to the point of jealousy. This is not real love. It is a touch of the emotion fear added to a conditional love relationship that is based on one-upmanship. It is the fear that there is only so much love to go around and that if another gets a great deal of love, then you might not get enough. Love is Spirit and Love is perfect and limitless. When you can release ideas and feelings about advantages and disadvantages and come to desire that good come to all, you are exercising your faculty of love.

Let's look at another aspect of love -- that of the magnetic, attracting power of love. Gravity is love. The love of mother earth draws all things to it. You, too, are Love and gravity, and you draw anything to you which you love. If you love a person or object, you draw them to you. You can even draw negative conditions, because you subconsciously love them. It is amazing how little we consciously use the magnetizing power of love. It is mostly utilized unconsciously. This is unfortunate, because we understand our subconscious so little that we cannot predict what we will draw to us. The beautiful thing about developing the awareness of love as a magnetizing, attracting power is that you can deliberately start loving that which you want to experience in your life. To love someone is to see your oneness with them. To love someone is to desire that only good come to them. To love someone is to draw them to you and experience them spiritually, whether they are physically present or not. To love prosperity is the drawing of prosperity into your life. To love health is to draw health into your life. To love a car is to draw it into your living experience. If any of these things are drawn into your life for the purpose of personal ego advantage over another, it is not Love. Love, like gravity, pulls things together with abundance and prosperity for all.

There is one last quality to be considered about this great gift of Love. Love is the great harmonizer of the universe. It is spiritual ointment for chaos and confusion. As it draws things together, it does it in a harmonious manner. If you are in a chaotic situation, you can direct love to the situation, and harmony will be restored. When you direct your love you are free of lesser emotional entanglements and and are capable of seeing the truth underlying all conditions. This insight and understanding puts your consciousness at ease which automatically puts the conditions at ease. In this sense, Love brings freedom. When you love someone, you free him. When you love a situation, you free it. When people and conditions are free, they are receptive to the natural harmony of the universe. Your ability to love restores the natural harmony of the universe. Your ability to love restores the natural harmony that underlies apparent chaos.

Love is a spiritual gift, an ability to direct the power of God for earthly good. It is important to exercise this ability for two reasons: first, for the good it does in harmonizing, attracting, and unifying, and second, for the development of your personal awareness of this magnificent gift of God. Remember, emotions come and go, but Love is never changing. Still yourself toward Love to the point of fulfillment. Then direct it generously, enabling peace to be restored on earth.

Love

SCRIPTURE

"They shall appear that love thee." (Ps. 122:6)
"By this shall all ye know me that ye are my disciples, if ye have love one to another." (Jn. 13:35)
"If ye keep my commandments, ye shall abide in love." (Jn. 15:10)
"Thou shalt love thy neighbor as thyself." (Ro. 13:9)

QUESTIONS

1. What is the result of your feeling nature when you are out of balance?
2. What is the result in your thinking nature when you are out of balance?
3. Is love an emotion?
4. What is your motive in loving others?
5. What is the difference between conditional and unconditional love?
6. Do you have emotional needs that must be met?
7. Explain oneness with all.
8. Can you see with your feeling nature?
9. Should good come to all or only the deserving?
10. Can someone have an advantage over you?
11. What is jealousy?
12. What is gravity?
13. How does love harmonize?
14. How is love related to freedom?

DENIAL

There is no absence of love, no sense of separateness in my life.

AFFIRMATION

The law of God is drawing all that I desire with good for all in peace and harmony.

POWER

POWER   is my ability to change and build consciousness.

POWER   is my ability to choose thoughts and feelings.

POWER   is my ability to transform energy from one
         plane to another.

37

PREVIEW

1. POWER is the ability to transform energy from one plane to another.

2. Silence, thought, word, and manifestation are stages of POWER in action.

3. POWER is the ability to change thoughts and feelings.

4. POWER is not for controlling others.

Every attribute of God is an attribute of man because man is in the image and likeness of his Father. But it is important to remember that each attribute that God has implanted in you is an ability you have with which to build consciousness. Each has a definite function, and you have an advantage in life if you understand these functions. In consciousness development, you need the ability to move spiritual energy about. You need to rid yourself of certain characteristics and add new ones. You will find yourself manifesting God's energy into homes, clothing, food, and then upgrading them. This ability to transform energy from one plane to another is called Power. God is absolute Power, and your ability to draw upon God as Power allows you to transform solids into liquids, ideas into bridges, and thoughts into buildings. This is your ability to heal, change your environment, and draw your good.

Of course, God is Spirit. But we often forget that man, too, is Spirit. So remembering that man is Spirit and perfect, we can lay claim to any good. When it is realized within and accepted in consciousness, divine energy rearranges itself to form into outer manifestation according to the new inner realization. Man's gift of Power is quickened through mental contact with its source, which is silence. One makes contact by turning in silence to pure Power.

Pure power is silence. Just as Strength is stillness, Power is silence. Strength is expended when you convert it into movement and actions. Power is expended when you convert it into vibrations or the Word. When you give the Word, you name the form which Spirit will take. Divine energy becomes anything you come to believe, so it is important to watch your thoughts, beliefs, and words very carefully. You are building a consciousness through the power you give them.

Silence, thought, word, and manifestation are stages of Power in action. In the silence there is no vibration. It is God as absolute Power awaiting your need to be recognized by you. A thought enters your head as you draw upon the Silence, and it registers in your consciousness as a vibration. The lower the frequency of the vibration, the more pure the thought is. The rate of vibration is determined by your consciousness and your spiritual development. This is why meditation and relaxation are so closely aligned. It is a recognized fact that the lowering of your thought waves elevates your creativity and spiritual awareness. Anger and fear throw you into a very high pitch, while love and assurance lower the level of vibration. After a thought enters your mind, you direct it as the Word. Silence is your pure Power. Thought is your formed Power, and the Word is your expressed Power which becomes manifest. It is vital that you realize what you are doing when you send your thoughts forth into the race consciousness and the world. You are literally shaping and forming the conditions in which you live. According to your consciousness, the world is being sustained. But the wonderful thing to realize is that you can change your environment and the world by elevating your thinking. If you permit thoughts to be formed which are of extremely low frequency, very spiritual, such as Love, Wisdom, and Understanding, you create a very spiritual atmosphere.

It benefits you to daily silence yourself and attune yourself with Spirit, so that you can serve as one who channels these qualities into the earth's atmosphere. Directing your love thoughts to a person is exactly the same as giving radiation treatments. You are actually radiating low spiritual frequencies toward the consciousness of that dear soul. As a spiritual being himself, he will sense the added spiritual thrust and may choose to be affected by your love. The power you have directed his way can alter his consciousness. If he allows these lower frequencies to act as his guide and way-shower, he will alter his vibrations according to this new level of love. Perhaps he had never before experienced such frequencies of love. You have served as a healer if he benefits from the power you have directed his way. Of course, you are automatically benefitted when you allow yourself to be used to this end. Such power moving through your consciousness transforms you into one who is very closely aligned to the Silence. Then a remarkable result occurs in your life. You accomplish so much more with less effort. More

40

happens as a result of your thought and the direction of your word. You end up doing less on the outer but effecting more.

Once again we come to the subject of the thinking nature and the feeling nature. With every spiritual gift we must recognize the importance of the balance between the thoughts and the feelings behind them. Of course, perfect balance between these two adds the quality of strength to whichever power we are considering. The result is strong faith, strong judgement, strong imagination, and so on. In your gift of Power, you need the element of strength as well. You need to be firmly seated in silence, not easily pulled off center. So, balance plays an important role in Power. Power is your ability to choose your thoughts and feelings. Most people don't realize this fact, but it is nevertheless true. You have the choice over anger, fear, compassion, tenderness, bigotry, attitudes, and beliefs. Unfortunately, you have been programmed with sets of ideas and emotions that have been repeated so many times that they are deeply ingrained. One of these beliefs is that it is difficult to change patterns of thoughts and feelings. This is not true. The truth is that most people basically do not want to change. But the ability to change, nevertheless, is there. There is an easy experiment you can make. The next time you are angry, crack a joke or simply choose to start smiling. You will immediately change the direction of your emotions. You may not want to, and you may feel a surrendering involved, but if you have the courage, you can instantaneously alter your emotions. Another experiment you can make is to alter your thinking when you are thinking that there is no hope. Right in the heart of a negative atmosphere, you can take hold of thoughts of hope and prosperity, and things will change.

You may wonder why you don't do it more often, since it is so simple to choose positive thoughts and feelings. It is because you haven't realized that you have had such Power at your disposal. Another reason is because of homeostasis in the human animal. Your body as a mechanism has a balancing system built into it. That is why it automatically heals itself. But this same homeostasis seeks to keep your consciousness at its present level. You as a human animal do not want change from the familiar. If the familiar is negative, you will have to overcome homeostasis to turn to the positive. But in any case, it is not difficult. It is a matter of wanting and remembering to choose new ways. Remember, by choosing compassion where you would normally choose impatience, you alter your consciousness. The lower frequencies heal your consciousness and develop a higher norm, or homeostasis, in your consciousness.

The greatest misconception about your gift of Power is the belief that it is to be used over other people. Your consciousness is greatly troubled if you are controlling and manipulating others. It is a sign of weakness, lack of balance, and fear. The danger comes when your attention is being constantly pulled to outer people and conditions rather than to the source of your power. This results in wars and a sense of "might makes right". A sense of separateness from your God manifests in your consciousness, and all responsibility for inner adjustments and spiritual development is abandoned. Your well-being never depends on others, so it is useless to manipulate people. Place your attention on the way you use your thought and word and how closely they are aligned to the Silence. This is how you develop your awareness of Power, not by controlling others.

Meditation and prayer are very low-frequency communications with God. Meditation is turning to the Silence to receive the inspiration needed to build awareness. Prayer is specific thought forms moving in your mind for perfect resolutions. Some people claim to be able to go beyond these levels and actually enter the Silence. If this is so, they have a rich, wonderful responsibility to mankind. They are capable of being channels of peace on earth, which is a form of Silence on earth. In any case, we can all assist in reducing useless noisemaking and hate vibrations. Silence neutralizes noise just as light neutralizes darkness. Say, "I love you," to someone who is angry with you and witness the effect on his behavior. On the other hand, you can say, "I hate you," to someone who is peaceful, and he is likely to be disturbed.

We must recognize our wonderful gift of Power as a spiritual tool in consciousness development and draw upon it to bring more spiritual awareness into the consciousness of mankind.

SCRIPTURE

"Ye shall receive Power, after that the Holy Ghost is come upon you." (Ac. 1:8)
"So mightily grew the word of God and prevailed." (Ac. 19:20)

"In all these things we are more than conquerors through him that loved us." (Ro. 8:37)
"God hath not given us the spirit of fear; but of power, and of love, and of sound mind." (2 Tim. 1:7)
"The word of God is quick, and powerful." (He. 4:12)

QUESTIONS

1. What is meant by transforming energy from one plane to another?
2. Is God at high-frequency levels?
3. How do you build or alter your consciousness?
4. What are the differences between Silence, thought, word, and manifestation?
5. Can you affect the consciousness of another?
6. How do you keep from depleting your Power?
7. Should your spiritual gifts be used separately from one another?
8. Do you really want to change?
9. Do you have choice over your thoughts?
10. Do you have choice over your emotions?
11. Is controlling others a sign of power?
12. What is prayer?
13. What is meditation?

DENIAL

No person or condition has power over my life.

AFFIRMATION

Divine Power is moving through me now, uplifting me, and changing my life.

44

IMAGINATION

IMAGINATION *is my ability to give shape and form to unformed mental energy.*

IMAGINATION *is vision beyond appearances.*

PREVIEW

1. IMAGINATION is the eye of the consciousness.

2. IMAGINATION gives shape, form, and color to unformed mental energy.

3. IMAGINATION is the projector of your potentials.

4. IMAGINATION releases overloaded mental and emotional energy.

5. IMAGINATION is vision beyond appearances.

The source of all is pure spiritual energy. Some call it God; some call it Divine Mind. Whatever you call it, you know that it is invisible and that it takes faith to draw from this invisible source to make it visible and useful to you. But there is another gift from God other than faith that is a wonderful spiritual tool in determining what the various potentials are that you should be drawing upon. Imagination is the eye of your consciousness. It is your ability to perceive the limitless possibilities of your good. It is that point of your consciousness where you can see and picture your desire. Even though that which you desire is still invisible, you can see it with your mind's eye. When you combine the use of faith with imagination, you see and know. It is only a matter of time from that point until your desire becomes an object in existence.

Imagination also gives shape, form, and color to unformed mental energy. As you perceive that which you need, you actually give it form. You have

46

the ability to shape, form, and then rearrange divine energy until it is the perfect answer to your need. Your emotions affect its coloring, and as you change your feelings about your need, you alter its coloring. Let's say you need a typewriter. You have in mind a small portable because you feel that you have a limited budget and that, at this time, it is the most practical. A friend hears about your need and insists that you must settle for no less than a grand table model with all the automatic features. He points out the fact that it is an investment in your future and that money should be no object. For the first time you consider a larger model, but as he describes the typewriter that he has in mind, you see that it is even more elaborate than you had imagined. You become excited over the idea of actually owning such a marvelous machine. You even picture it on your desk. Finally, you decide this is what you really want. At this point, spiritual-mental energy is forming into definition and is seeking the way to enter your living experience. You have established it in consciousness, and whether or not it comes into your life depends upon your use of your spiritual gifts.

If you exercise strength, you stick with this idea until it becomes firmly established in your consciousness. If you exercise faith, the typewriter begins to move toward you, transforming itself from the fourth dimension to the third. If you exercise wisdom, ideas unfold in your consciousness which instruct you on how you may obtain the typewriter quickly and with ease. If you still yourself toward the Christ within you as Divine Imagination, you give the shape, form, and color of your perfect typewriter to mental energy.

As a matter of clarification, spiritual energy and mental energy are one and the same. These terms are interchangeable, but to avoid confusion, it is necessary for you to know that Divine Mind, Spirit, thought substance, Father, spiritual energy, mental energy, and God all refer to the Source of all that is. Even stillness and silence are referring to the one source. It is from this source that imagination shapes and forms. It is from this Source that strength is drawn. It is from this source that love is drawn. It is from this source that all power vibrates and wisdom expresses. God is so vast, yet so simple, that He, or it, remains unnamable. That is why so many definitions are given to the Source. Man's imagination is still trying to give form to the formless, definition to the undefinable. The wonderful paradox of it all is that as we draw from the invisible, creating the manifest world, we are being transformed into the invisible fourth dimension ourselves.

Now, let us consider the imagination as a projector. Assuming that in your mind you have formed a definite clear thought as to what your need is, your imagination will project it into your life experience. The screen of life is the third dimension. You, as a human being, perceive through your five senses in the third dimension. For you to see and comprehend, as a human being, objects need to have height, width, depth, smell, taste, sound, all the properties that can be recorded through your body temple. Of course, as a spiritual being, you pick up far more, but you are still in need of the third dimension screen for most of your living experience. So, if there is an object or event which is still in the invisible, you can imagine what it would be like even before it manifests in the third dimension. If you don't like the way it projects, you can easily rearrange it while it is still invisible. If you approve of what you project, you can hold to the image until faith draws it out of the invisible.

There is another wonderful function of your imagination that, if properly understood, can serve as a great benefit to your spiritual development. Imagination can serve to release overloaded mental and emotional energy. Sometimes, too much information or emotion is poured into your consciousness before you are equipped to handle it. For instance, if you had a near auto accident, your imagination might picture all sorts of sordid scenes, even though nothing actually happened. The event might produce more emotional input than your consciousness can handle. Therefore, you may find yourself in the midst of all sorts of wild imaginings. If you are aware of what is taking place, you can release these imaginings, recognizing them for what they are. Unfortunatly, some people scare themselves to death, involving themselves into the process of fantasizing or worrying that these are signs of things to come. It is merely the expending of excess emotional energy through imagination. Rightly understood, it is a safety valve that prevents you from going off balance. Wrongly understood, these images can be held through fear and projected into the third dimension.

This releasing process that takes place through the imagination can take place while awake or asleep. If you awaken from a nightmare, you can honestly say, "Thank goodness, that is out of my system". If the process continues, it is nothing to concern yourself about. The emotion is still spending itself through your imagination. If you bless it and release it, your consciousness will finish with its re-evaluation of the incident, and peace will be restored.

Your imagination is vision beyond appearances. There is something in you that knows that your possibilities are not limited to what appears before you now. It even knows that your concepts are not the extent of what you understand. It is the Christ in you communicating to you through your imagination. Your imagination is another avenue, other than intuition, through which God communicates to you. Once again it is used as a projector. But rather than being projected into the third dimension, it is projected onto the screen of your consciousness. You receive the communication as a vision, a dream, or a revelation. New ways, new insights, and clues to your subconscious are revealed to you in symbols through your imagination. The significance of these symbols is revealed as you meet life's challenges and opportunities. As they are unclothed, you will receive directions and experience release at the same time. Your communications from God help to make sense out of a world of limited appearances.

A question that arises in regards to the use of imagination is that of outlining. Should you be specific in your imaginings so that you get a good, clear picture of what you want, or should you leave the details to God and work with generalities. There is the concern that being too specific may limit or block what God has in mind for you. Here is the answer to the question. Your greatest need is God-awareness. Every lesser need that appears is part of a divine plan that is unfolding toward the realization of this spiritual awareness. It is perfectly all right to be specific about picturing your good because you are always willing to alter the picture according to new revelation. If your true motive is spiritual growth, you will never willfully cling to anything that is less than good for you. For instance, if you feel the need to travel across the country, and you picture yourself flying in an airplane, you are becoming one with the journey. But, if someone hands you free train tickets, you should be open to the incident. You have not failed in the constructive use of your imagination by the mere fact that they were not airplane tickets. There is some reason you are meant to make the journey, and the method of transportation is revealing itself to you. Be receptive to God's will so that you may be led. Just because the picture is altered, you should not be discouraged from ever picturing again. The picturing simulates spiritual activity within, and the new inner activity might trigger greater alternatives in your picturing. Whenever you picture your good, don't limit yourself by being receptive to nothing better. Have the courage to be specific, yet remain open to new guidance and inspiration.

Never disqualify your imagination by saying,"It's only my imagination". It is a spiritual gift from God which assists you in developing awareness. It is the link between your present consciousness and your undreamed-of possibilities.

SCRIPTURE

"God said, let us make man in our image." *(Ge. 1:26)*

"As we have borne the image of the earthly, we shall also bear the image of the heavenly." (1 Co. 8:4)
"The Lord searcheth all hearts, and understandeth all the imaginations and the thoughts." (1 Ch. 28:9)

QUESTIONS

1. How is Faith related to imagination?
2. How do your emotions affect the use of imagination?
3. How is imagination a time saver?
4. What are the various names given to the source of all your good?
5. How is imagination a projector?
6. What does it project to?
7. Are terrible scenes predictions of disaster?
8. How is your imagination a communication system with God?
9. What is meant by outlining?

DENIAL

There are no limitations or boundaries in my life.

AFFIRMATION

I see wonderful new people, situations, and supply coming to me now in my spiritual development.

UNDERSTANDING

UNDERSTANDING *is my ability to know that God
stands under all things.*

UNDERSTANDING *is my knowing how to accomplish.*

UNDERSTANDING *is knowing with my heart.*

53

PREVIEW

1. UNDERSTANDING is your ability to know that God stands under all things.

2. UNDERSTANDING is your knowing how to accomplish.

3. UNDERSTANDING is knowing with your heart.

Whenever you meet something that you can't understand, it simply means that you can't see the order, the good, or any purpose to it. In other words, you can't see how God stands under this situation. But that doesn't mean that God doesn't stand under the situation; it only appears to be that way to you. In reality, God stands under all things as principle. There is some principle in effect that you need to understand before you can have mental satisfaction. But let us assume there is a situation where there seems to be no rhyme nor reason. Is there any way to find peace of mind and heart without understanding all the details? The answer is yes. You can still yourself to Divine Understanding. This allows you to realize that there is a spiritual law in effect even though you can't detect it at the moment. Jesus said, "Ye believe because you have seen, but blessed are they who believe and who have not see". This is the exercising of understanding. It is trusting in God when you would have been otherwise skeptical.

A skeptic feels that things aren't as good as they should be, but that doesn't mean he doesn't want to be convinced. We all want to be convinced. You are a spiritual being, living in a spiritual world, governed by spiritual laws. This is not always apparent to one who is governed by appearances. He constantly asks for proof and stays in one spot until he finds it. This is called, "seeing is believing". Divine understanding is developed by declaring that God as principle stands under all things and that within all things, there is good.

It is important always to remember that understanding is more than cognition of the mind. It is more than impulses moving through your brain. It is Spirit in action, Divine Energy pouring through your consciousness as understanding. This is why you can move forward in an assured manner even though you don't have all the answers. Divine Understanding allows you to move on faith.

Does this mean you can build a house without knowing how? Does this mean you don't need to know any facts or figures or dimensions in constructing a building? Can you build such a building without understanding what you are doing? No, it doesn't mean that. In fact, there is very little you can accomplish in your life experience without understanding what you are doing. Understanding is your knowing how to accomplish. It is important to understand the principles that underlie building construction if you are going to build a house. There is a principle of stress, of support, of balance, of management, of economics. When you understand these principles, you use them as unfailing laws with which to build your building. It is through your understanding of these principles that you can accomplish the project.

This may seem in contradiction with an earlier

statement. How can it be said that you can move forward through understanding without having all the answers and also say that it is very important to understand the underlying principles? Here is the answer. In the long run you do get the answers. Most of the time you move ahead knowing what you are doing and how to do it. But there are times when you feel you should move ahead, yet you do not have the know-how. You don't understand how to go about it. This brings you to a very important decision. Are you blocked by the lack of understanding or do you still yourself to Divine Understanding? According to appearances, you have moved to a point that is beyond your present understanding. But need you stop? No, you do not stop. Instead, you proceed to silence and stillness which is the strongest and most powerful position you can take. Stilling yourself to Divine Understanding reminds you that God is standing under the situation and is but awaiting your request for truth, insight, and revelation. By relying on God to give you the answers step by step, you are developing your awareness of Divine Understanding and accomplishing the task at the same time. Perhaps you do not know how to accomplish, but Divine Understanding does.

Basically, this is what takes place. As you move forward, declaring Divine Understanding, the underlying principles come to your mind. When this takes place, you can apply the facts to the principles, and miracles take place. You suddenly become aware of the limitless materials that have been at your disposal, overlooked, up until now.

When you still yourself, you are placing God first in all affairs. Whenever you ask God to take over, you release your limited point of view. This released limited point of view is replaced with the understanding of some underlying principle, and eventually it moves through your consciousness into your conscious awareness. So, whenever you are blocked by not knowing how, let God show you how. Remember, ask, and it shall be given you. Seek, and ye shall find. Knock, and it shall be opened unto you. Seek Divine Understanding and then ask, knock, inquire, and proceed according to the principles that are revealed to you.

Understanding is knowing with your heart. You can have all the facts, and they may be true, but they are not the Truth. Facts can be gathered and evaluated, but the Truth can be felt and lived. Sometimes you can understand how to accomplish without all the facts. You have a knowing that tells you that something is possible, a feeling of rightness. This is illustrated by one who picks up a musical instrument and plays it with little or no instruction. He simply knows how to play the instrument. Some people "understand" animals and can train them with great ease. They seem to have a feeling for them. A person can walk into a house and know that it is meant to be for him. He has a feeling for it and knows that it will be his no matter what obstacles present themselves. The common ingredient in all these cases is love. Understanding moves quickly on love. You can accomplish quickly and easily in a loving situation. Understanding is stifled in the absence of love. A person can completely understand his craft, but if he is under severe criticism and hatred, he can barely perform. He has lost a sense of rightness about the entire thing.

The perfect combination, of course, is understanding with the head and understanding with the heart at the same time. You can retain facts and knowledge in the head, but without heart knowing, you won't know that God stands under all that you accomplish.

God wants only good for you and He is the sustaining, loving force that upholds the universe. God's divine plan for you is to have you accept all His good. When you understand this, you understand what is behind all incidents that take place in your worldly experience. All your experiences, whether they appear to be positive or negative, are part of God's plan for your good. This knowingness comes through your feeling nature or your heart. When you accept the fact that everything is working together for good, you understand how to accomplish. All fear is removed; confidence is restored; and understanding is established.

To understand someone is to love him. No matter how negative a person might be, if you understand him, you love him. You see the Christ in him if you understand him. You grow in understanding when you exercise it in those areas where you don't seem to understand. For instance: you offer understanding to someone you really don't understand. Even though you can't grasp why he is behaving in a certain manner you affirm that he is a spiritual being and needs your love and understanding. When you do this, you begin to understand his behavior in no time at all.

There is only one real thing you have to understand. The truth that stands under all changing facts and circumstances is God. There is only one power and presence in the universe and it stands under all things. To know this is to have spiritual understanding.

SCRIPTURE

"Wisdom is the principal thing; therefore get wisdom: and with all thy getting get understanding." (Pr. 4:7)
"In malice be ye children, but in understanding be men." (1 Co. 14:20)
"Through Faith we understand." (He. 11:3)

QUESTIONS

1. What is principle?
2. Does God stand under all negative conditions?
3. Should you always stop when you don't understand how to proceed?
4. Are facts unimportant in life?
5. Where does one find spiritual understanding?
6. How is release related to understanding?
7. What is the difference between true facts and the Truth?
8. Does love facilitate understanding?
9. Can you understand someone and hate him at the same time?

DENIAL

There is no condition or lack of information that can prevent me from accomplishing.

AFFIRMATION

God stands under all things and the perfect out-working is being revealed to me now.

WILL

WILL   *is my ability to be willing toward God.*

WILL   *is always seeking the good for all.*

WILL   *is my directive power that determines character formation.*

PREVIEW

1. WILL is your ability to be willing toward God.

2. You must choose willingness over willfulness.

3. WILL is always seeking good for all.

4. The WILL is the great permission-giver of your consciousness.

5. WILL determines character formation.

One has a tremendous overcoming when he is able to be willing toward God. But the development of this ability comes through the many surrenderings of old ways. No matter how well you understand spiritual laws, if you are not willing to adhere to them, they are not useful to you. If you are not willing to forgive, for instance, the cleansing activity of forgiveness cannot move through you. Why would one not be willing toward God and spiritual principles when there is such a benefit in becoming so? The answer is fear! Fear of change from that which is familiar holds one fixed in a rigid position. So, one must overcome fear of change in order to become willing toward God. You feel very vulnerable as you move through these overcomings, even to the point of losing security in your feeling nature. But it is important to loosen the grip of your present feeling nature so you can take a new grip. Once you get a firm hold on your new level of consciousness, you become confident and secure there, until it is time to move on once more. It is up to you to develop your ability to become more and more willing toward God. You need to become less and less dependent on old ways.

Actually, you must choose willingness over willfulness. It comes right down to "Thy will, not my will". Willingness is always constructive in your consciousness building. Willfulness is always destructive. Willfulness lacks the courage to depend on God for having needs met and, at the same time, ignores spiritual laws. It includes self-determination and takes credit for all that is accomplished. Willfulness acts according to facts that are presented in the outer, not according to intuition and spiritual guidance.

Willingness acknowledges the outer facts but moves according to inner instruction. Willingness benefits from both directions because it recognizes them as being one. It takes great courage to be willing toward God. Encourage yourself. Put courage in where facts seem negative. Put courage into your thinking and feeling when you are shaken by God's instruction. It is not always easy to be obedient to your inner instructions, but you must be courageous in spite of the facts. When you choose willingness over willfulness, the facts adjust into the revelation that God wants only good for you.

In John 5:30, we read Jesus' words, "I seek not mine own will, but the will of the Father which hath sent me". But, what is the will of the Father? What is God's will seeking? Will is always seeking good for all! So, as long as you are seeking good for all, with harm to no one, you are moving according to God's will. If you are in a situation where you are seeking good, you must ask yourself whether or not your goal includes a disadvantage to someone else. If it does, you are being willful. Until you see a wonderful possibility for everyone, keep listening to your Father. There is a way trying to reveal itself to you. If appearances seem to say, "It's either you or the other guy who will benefit," you are still holding the limited view of willfulness.

This brings us to a very important point. There is the mistaken belief that pain and suffering are part of God's will for individuals and mankind. This is using God as a scapegoat. Pain and suffering are results of man's breaking the law of his own highest good. When you choose not to adhere to spiritual principles, you find yourself in limiting conditions. If you use poor judgement and climb a mountain without the proper gear and training, you are likely to have an accident. It is not God's will that you have an accident; you have simply not paid attention to the laws of safety and gravity. God is not punishing you because you have not obeyed his laws; the reaction is simply in accordance with the dependability and accuracy of the laws of safety and gravity.

The belief that God punishes causes untold suffering and confusion. If you believe that you are being punished, you believe that you have done something bad. This leads to the belief that you are a bad person. This is a threat to your very self-esteem. It is important to realize that making a mistake in breaking the law is not the same as being bad. You cannot be bad. You are good, as God is good. Being willful is not being bad. It is merely refusing to adhere to those divine principles which bring forth all good in your life. Being willing, on the other hand, leads you into the understanding that you are all good. Willingness leads you to the understanding that you have a loving Father and that it is His will that good comes to all.

Your will is the great permission-giver of your consciousness. It moves to action all the other spiritual gifts. No matter how much you understand your God-given gifts, if you are not willing to use them, they remain as potential only. A birthday gift isn't very exciting to you if you don't unwrap it. God gave you twelve spiritual gifts at birth, and, unless you unwrap them, you will not develop in consciousness. You must be willing to untie the ribbon and peel back the wrapping to discover these gifts. Then, as you use these gifts, you realize that they are all part of the one gift, your Christ-self.

No matter how much you understand love, you must give it permission over anger. You must give permission to strength over intolerance and discouragement. You must give permission to good judgement over irrational impulse. You must give permission to faith over appearances. These abilities are all at your command, but you must give the command. All things are within you. You manifest in your life whatever you give permission. You give permission to that which you give your attention. If you do not give your attention to your wonderful spiritual gifts, you cannot give them permission to move into expression in your life. The best way to give your attention to a particular gift is to silence yourself toward it. Silence yourself toward Strength, and divine energy will flow through you. Silence yourself toward Power, and you will feel your consciousness move to a higher level. Silence yourself toward Faith, and your good will flow from the invisible into your living experience.

If you are wondering which spiritual gift you should be giving permission to, I recommend you take this approach. Consider your most current challenge. Everyone is meeting some challenge at all times, or he is not growing. In considering your concerns over the challenge, check your list of twelve spiritual gifts. You will easily discern in which area you are out of balance. Place your attention on that gift. Meditate on it, and silence yourself toward that particular God-given ability. This activates it in your consciousness, and it is revealed to you how your challenge is meant to help you grow.

Will determines character formation. As you consciously choose the development of awareness of your specific gifts, you are actually determining the shape of your character. You are willing to become more loving, stronger, wiser, and more creative as you choose to give permission to these God-qualities to overcome your old self. You can become anything that you are willing toward. Instead of trying to escape from life's challenges, you can become more willing to grow into the greater good. Build your character. Your challenges are not pointing out your weakness. They are identifying for you those gifts in which you need to develop awareness. Don't meet these challenges in old ways. Turn to Christ within and meet the gift or the ability that will overcome the challenge through you. The result will be greater awareness of peace and harmony in your life.

SCRIPTURE

"Thy will be done in earth as it is in heaven." (Mat. 6:10)
"Father, if thou be willing, remove this cup from me: nevertheless not my will, but thine, be done." (Luke 22:42)
"My meat is to do the will of Him that sent me, and to finish His work." (Jn. 4:34)
"This is the Father's will which hath sent me, that of all which he hath given me, I should lose nothing." (John 6:39)

QUESTIONS

1. Does the understanding of spiritual laws necessarily build consciousness?
2. What blocks willingness?
3. What is the difference between willingness and willfulness?
4. What is the source of willingness?
5. What is the source of willfulness?
6. What is God's will for you personally?
7. Do your goals include good for everyone concerned?
8. Can God's will include suffering and pain?
9. Is there a bad part of you?
10. Do your other spiritual gifts depend upon will?
11. How do you give permission to one of your abilities?
12. How do you determine which gift you should be developing?

DENIAL

I release old ways, making room for new awareness.

AFFIRMATION

I am open, receptive, and willing to accept God's will.

ORDER

ORDER   is my ability to develop consciousness in proper sequence -- mind, body, and affairs.

ORDER   is my adjustment and harmony in health, illumination, and prosperity.

ORDER   is my ability to keep "God first" in my continuous development.

69

PREVIEW

1. ORDER is your ability to develop consciousness in proper sequence -- mind, body, and affairs.

2. ORDER is your adjustment and harmony in health, illumination, and prosperity.

3. ORDER eliminates generalizations.

4. A divine plan is unfolding through you now.

5. ORDER is your ability to keep God first in your continuous development.

You are on a journey, a journey of consciousness development and transformation. But when you are going someplace, you should always know where you are going and how you are getting there. In consciousness development, the goal is the attainment of the Christ-consciousness. The way you attain it is through adhering to spiritual principles. So you have your goal and the way. Your vehicle is a physical body which is propelled by your thoughts and feelings. And, of course, your thoughts and feelings originate from Source, God. In their pure form, thoughts and feelings are Divine Wisdom and Divine Love, but, as they are filtered through your consciousness, they manifest as personal thoughts and personal feelings. It is best that you keep your mind, body, and affairs in perfect order, so that this wonderful balance of thoughts and feelings keeps you focused on your goal, Christ-awareness. But there are times when things get out of order. A personal negative thought can result in a negative belief, and the natural unfoldment becomes disturbed. Emotions pick up the disturbance, and chaos results throughout your entire consciousness.

Order is your ability to develop consciousness in proper sequence. Your sequence is different from that of all other souls. What you are meant to experience, no one else experiences in just the same way. This uniqueness is expressed through your mind, through your body, and through your affairs. If your affairs are out of order, it is a reflection that your thinking is out of order. If your body is out of order, it is a reflection that your emotions are out of order. If you can't detect how you are out of order, you can still yourself to Divine Order and permit it to affect your consciousness. Upon invitation, the Christ in you transforms your consciousness from confusion to order. Soon it is revealed to you what your first step should be in establishing order in your affairs. You have made many conclusions in your life and some of them are incorrect. It is these incorrect conclusions that must be disconnected and rewired, so to speak.

Order is your adjustment and harmony in health, illumination, and prosperity. Your body temple is a human mechanism which contains Spirit as your soul. As a mechanism, it is completely obedient to your consciousness. Like a computer, if it receives improper programming, it will go out of order or break down. Divine Order restores in you that which is out of sequence. Let us assume that you are physically ill. Perhaps you are doing things in your life that are not adherent to spiritual principles. Perhaps you are holding thoughts and feelings that are causing short circuits in your consciousness. Your body, too, will short circuit, because it is completely a product of your consciousness. A band-aid might help, but the real correction needs to come from within.

If a person puts his job before his family, his sub-conscious might tell him that he is out of order. Soon the guilt will cause a short circuit which can result in an illness that will keep him home with his family. If he stills himself to Divine Order, he will have revealed to him that which should come first. Remember this: whenever Order reveals to you which adjustments you need to make, you discover that there is more than enough time to do all things. Less time is necessary when things are in proper sequence. Many times people get out of order, thinking that they don't have time to accomplish everything. Divine Order will always reveal to you enough time to do all those things which you are meant to do. So, whenever you feel that you don't have enough time to do it all, still yourself to Divine Order.

Order eliminates generalizations. Too often, people can't identify the problem or the solution. You have twelve beautiful spiritual gifts, each for a specific purpose in consciousness building. It is important to understand the twelve, so that you know which ones to call upon in meeting a challenge. It is orderly to resolve hate with love, chaos with order, frustration with strength, ignorance with judgement, and so on. Many people conclude that every time they have a challenge or desire, they need more faith. This simply is not true. Perhaps bringing something from the invisible is not the issue at all. Perhaps it is a matter of judgement or love. Spirit is Perfect Order, and you must be orderly in your acknowledgment of it. If you find difficulty in discovering where you are out of balance, listen to your wording in describing the problem. If you are making statements like, "I don't understand," then still yourself to Divine Understanding. If your wording infers impatience and weakness, still yourself toward Divine Strength. If your comments reveal that you can't see where the resolution will come from, still yourself toward Faith. Be specific, and witness the release of the most powerful inner movement your consciousness has ever experienced.

A divine plan is unfolding through you now. You have a magnificent purpose on this planet earth, and your realization of this purpose is coming in a special way. It is your contribution to the uplifting of mankind. But this plan needs to unfold in an orderly manner that will result in consciousness development for you. So, two things are being accomplished at the same time. On the one hand, the plan is showing you how to serve, and on the other, you are growing in awareness.

In your development there is no limitation as to time, space, or means, because God is infinite with neither beginning nor end. But all this infiniteness is a little mind-boggling to you as an individual. Therefore, you have a wonderful spiritual gift which translates this infinite time, space, and means into when, where, and how. It is necessary for you as a human to understand when you are meant to do something, where to do it, and how. Stilling yourself to

Order releases all this infiniteness into your consciousness as answers to when, where, and how.

An interesting thing to note is that it takes place in your consciousness instantly. Just like judgement, order is one of those instantaneous actions that immediately starts the outworking of your affairs. It might take a while for it to appear on the outer, but it begins with your first affirmative declaration of order.

Order is your ability to keep "God first" in your continuous development. You might think these explanations of order are too complex to comprehend when one is facing chaos and confusion. How does one find order and proper sequence under pressure? Just say, "God first". That's all it takes. That starts your consciousness accepting the proper connections and sequences of information and inspiration. If you can place God first in any situation, that situation has no choice but to fall into order. If you place personal love first, then step 3 might follow step 7, and step 2 might follow step 88. But, if you put God first, step 2 falls into line and immediately precedes step 3. Step 4 follows, and the orderly revelations continue. The minute your priority moves from God to money, lust, or ego, your sequence has permission to slip into chaos. If you feel you don't know where to begin or which step to take next, insist on God first in your life and the mystery will begin to unravel.

There is no coincidence in Spirit other than Divine Coincidence. You are in your right place, at the right time, studying the perfect lesson right now. You are in perfect order.

Order

SCRIPTURE

"The steps of a good man are ordered by the Lord."
(Ps. 37:23)
"Order my steps in thy word." (Ps. 119:133)
"First the blade, then the ear, after that the full corn
in the ear." (Mk. 4:28)
"The times of this ignorance God winked at; but now
commandeth all men everywhere to repent." (Ac. 17:30)
"Let all things be done decently and in order." (1 Co. 14:40)

QUESTIONS

1. What is your greatest goal?
2. How do you achieve it?
3. Should your mind, body and affairs follow the same sequence as others?
4. Is there enough time to get through all the things you need to do?
5. Is it important to be clear as to which spiritual gifts you are calling upon?
6. Are you meant to do something important for mankind?
7. Into what terms does order translate time, space, and means?
8. How long does it take to establish order?
9. What is the quickest way to establish proper sequence of events?
10. Is coincidence accidental?

DENIAL

Chaos and confusion are hereby eliminated from my life.

AFFIRMATION

God is first in my life and is revealing my very next step, right now.

ZEAL

ZEAL   is my ability to move forward through spiritual motivation.

ZEAL   results in my enthusiasm and joy.

ZEAL   is my affirmative impulse of existence.

PREVIEW

1. ZEAL is needed for spiritual progress.

2. ZEAL results in joy and enthusiasm.

3. ZEAL harmonizes you with the universe.

4. ZEAL is the opposite of nostalgia and apathy.

Too often being dedicated to God's work is considered to be a sorrowful, heavy experience which is full of martyrdom. This is a mistaken idea. If a person feels this way about serving, he is not drawing upon his God-given gift of zeal. Zeal generates pleasant, spiritual motivation for consciousness development. Zeal is your ability to move forward in developing awareness and loving it at the same time.

You are aware that man has evolved and improved physically. Throughout the years, his body has adapted and grown stronger through proper nutrition. But man has had spiritual progress as well. This has been motivated by a desire to grow. It is a pleasant, low-key desire which serves as fuel for motivation. It is proper nutrition which causes a warm, deep desire for soul food. Zeal is your spiritual appetite. Without it, you would neither care about spiritual progress, nor enjoy spiritual thoughts and feelings. Zeal is Spirit -- silent, still -- and is ever urging you onward to greater awareness of your Christ-self.

Zeal results in joy and enthusiasm. From silent zeal you draw joy, which is still quite low key and deep as a living experience. Joy is the first expression

of zeal and is the most usable form of zeal in the
human experience. Joy is the use of zeal at very low
frequency. Therefore, the mind and heart are not
confused, because these frequencies are easily
incorporated into spiritual activity. When you are
using zeal as joy, you have not entered that range
that is similar to physical pleasure and excitement.
Now, enthusiasm vibrates at a higher frequency
which resembles the vibrations of sensual pleasure.
There is nothing wrong with sensual pleasure in the
human experience unless it is confused with or
supercedes spiritual motivation. If it replaces zeal
or spiritual motivation in importance, it becomes a
threat to one's progress. It becomes a diversion.
Unfortunately, sensual pleasure has been labeled
bad and something to avoid. This is ridiculous. It is
merely a part of your animal nature that needs to be
kept in perspective. It is very useful in expressing
and spending less energy, but certainly it is not to
become the goal or a way of life. So we see zeal in its
various frequencies as silent zeal, joy, enthusiasm,
and we will add exuberance. They are all good and
have purpose. The closer one moves toward exuberance, the more the store of zeal is spent. If one feels
enthusiasm waning, it is time to return to the silence
and replenish himself just as one does with strength
and power. How wonderful to know there is no limit
to the source of your supply! But it is vital to keep
in mind that this almighty Source is meant to be
drawn upon for spiritual growth rather than just
pleasurable experiences. If you abuse your mind,
soul, and body, you are in for some drastic negative
experiences.

Zeal dissolves subconscious barriers and conscious beliefs. Without the desire to move forward, you could never overcome negative limiting beliefs or face hidden fears. There is nothing so fixed in your consciousness that zeal can't dissolve and overcome. Once fixed beliefs and fears are shattered, their very structure is exposed to the light of truth. There is no disease that can survive in light, and zeal is ever urging you onward into the light.

There is a rhythm to the universe. Call it the heart-beat of God or whatever, there are definite cycles and rhythms in nature, mankind, the universe, and Spirit. The oceans have high tide and low tide; the year has seasons; the heart contracts and relaxes. Zeal harmonizes you with the universe. When you are spiritually motivated, you need not strain in your development of consciousness. The very rhythm of all that is will literally carry you forward. This is your tuning in to the zeal that is all about you. When your motives are based upon fear and self-service, you have to make tremendous efforts to even keep up with life, so it is a great advantage to you to still yourself to the divine motivation of zeal. If you fall out of step with this rhythm, either you lose all incentive or you can speed up your activities into meaninglessness. In the first place, if you lose spiritual incentive, you are heading for an experience called depression. Out of panic, you may try to overcompensate by seeking outer excitement. This can result in excessive enthusiasm and exuberance to the point of complete exhaustion. This kind of energy spent on egotistical endeavors cannot move you beyond fears or negative beliefs. In fact it accomplishes the opposite. The minute you meet an obstacle, you crumble, believing that the obstacle is much more powerful than you. There is no joy found in this situation, only disillusionment.

There is no such thing as the absence of zeal. If you hear someone say that he has no enthusiasm, you may assume he is merely unaware that he has access to limitless zeal, joy, and enthusiasm. He is not consciously experiencing enthusiasm, but he has all he will ever need right now. If one feels the lack of zeal and enthusiasm, he feels apathetic. Zeal is the opposite of apathy, nostalgia, and regret. Apathy feeds on the grip of the past. The thought of past deeds, whether fondly or regretfully held onto, can grind your forward thrust to a halt. Turning to the past for pleasure or guilt stifles any joy or enthusiasm for God's divine plan for you. It is vital that you release the past and all the concerns that go with it, or else you cannot still yourself toward zeal. Memories that would hold your attention are noisy. There are two ways to deal with memories. They can drag you backwards so that you can escape the present, or you can bring them forward to experience in the "now" for spiritual purposes. The motive is the key, and, remember, zeal is spiritual motive.

Pleasant memories can be a "now" experience which can assist in inspiring you into drawing upon your spiritual gift of zeal. This is in useful cooperation with imagination. The motive is pure and legitimate. Constructive memories which align you with true joy are quite valuable to your present consciousness. But they must not become your goal. They are to serve as a launching pad for spiritual motivation. If, for instance, fond memories of your mother and father inspire strength, love, and wisdom in you and help you model your life in spiritual directions, you are utilizing zeal in you. If, on the other hand, you want to cling to the memory of your parents, feeling that everyone else is wicked and things just aren't as good as they used to be, you are escaping to the past.

Regret is a crippler of two of your spiritual gifts, judgement and zeal. In judgement, it feeds on poor choices, but in the case of zeal, it pulls the focus from "go forward" to "look back". In order to feel the affirmative impulse of the universe, you must focus forward. The Kingdom of Heaven is the realm of ever-expanding ideas, and to experience the Kingdom of Heaven, you must involve yourself in the process of expansion. Heaven is not a place. It is a process and an experience for you to enjoy. Your desire to expand in consciousness is motivated by Spirit as zeal.

With the use of any of your spiritual gifts, release is an important factor. Very often forgiveness is involved with release. With no forgiveness or release, you can't be free of past memories and regret. All forgiveness involves forgiving yourself in some way. Forgive yourself and still yourself toward zeal so you may be propelled beyond limited beliefs and fears.

SCRIPTURE

"The zeal of thine house hath eaten me up." (Ps. 69:9)
"The zeal of the Lord of hosts will perform this." (Is. 9:7)
"Whatsoever ye do, do it heartily, as to the Lord, and not unto men." (Col. 4:13)

Zeal

"It is good to be zealously affected always in a good thing." (Ga. 4:18)
"I press toward the mark for the prize of the high calling of God in Christ Jesus." (Ph. 3:14)

QUESTIONS

1. What are the outer expressions of zeal?
2. Should you be as enthusiastic as possible at all times?
3. Is sensual pleasure bad?
4. How do you move through subconscious barriers?
5. Does drawing upon and using zeal involve great effort?
6. Can you run out of zeal?
7. Is the use of memories bad?
8. What is the crippler of zeal?
9. How does release affect zeal?
10. Who is the most important person that you can forgive?

DENIAL

Discouragement and apathy are no longer a part of my consciousness.

AFFIRMATION

The zeal of God pours through me now as joy, enthusiasm, and exuberance!

RENUNCIATION

RENUNCIATION *is my ability to give a "NO" response to the untrue and undesirable.*

RENUNCIATION *helps me eliminate errors and expand good.*

RENUNCIATION *is to release and forgive as well as to let go of old thoughts.*

PREVIEW

1. RENUNCIATION is your ability to release negative thoughts, feelings, and beliefs from your consciousness.

2. RENUNCIATION is your ability to give a "no" response to negativity.

3. RENUNCIATION is your ability to forgive and release others.

4. RENUNCIATION creates a vacuum.

5. RENUNCIATION is entirely an inner process.

Renunciation has two main functions in your consciousness. They are both related to keeping your consciousness pure and uncluttered. These two functions are the avoiding of negativity and the elimination of negativity. We will deal with the latter first since it is the most commonly understood purpose of this incredible spiritual gift.

Renunciation is your ability to eliminate negative thoughts, feelings, and beliefs from your consciousness. Often you might discover that there is a fear in you that you need to have eliminated from your feeling nature. It might seem that this fear is closely tied to a very real outer threat and that the threat must be removed before the fear will go away. If you believe this, you are tied to outer conditions. In Spirit you can release the fear before the outer threat is removed and therefore eliminate any power that the condition has over you. If you are not afraid, you cannot be harmed. So it is vital to remove all fear from your consciousness. You may ask how one does this. One of the greatest ways to release fear or worry is to invite Spirit to remove it for you with the statement, "I let go, and I let God". Then, physically relax. Deliberately loosen your muscles and relax your concerns. To your delight, you will feel the tie that binds you to the outer condition loosen. Another very constructive way to eliminate a negative inner state is to still yourself toward the divine gift of renunciation. Find a place where you can be alone and be still and think of Divine Release. The very gift itself will activate in you, freeing you from the negative experience.

Your gift of renunciation takes things out of existence. Everything that is in existence has been brought forth through the affirmative power of faith or belief. It is drawn into existence from invisible spiritual energy. Renunciation does just the opposite. It takes it from existence back to harmless creative energy. When something negative is removed from existence, it is called a cleansing of consciousness. Bible symbology illustrates this with the flood of Noah and the parting of the Red Sea. The flood took with it all the impurities of the world, and the closing of the sea removed all threats. This is why water baptism is used in preparation for receiving the Holy Spirit. There was a great deal of turmoil preceding the flood and the closing of the sea. Therefore, if there is a great deal of current turmoil in your life to the point that you feel overwhelmed, it is time for you to let go and let God. If you do, you will experience a personal cleansing, and your life will have new meaning. The negative forms will weaken in structure until they are reduced and returned to pure potential, which is waiting to be brought back into existence for good.

At one level of consciousness, you can eliminate negativity, but at a higher level you can avoid negativity. Renunciation is your ability to give a "no" response to negativity. It is your ability to reject that which is not of Spirit. Of course that which is not permitted to enter your consciousness does not have to be eliminated. It is a fabulous experience to observe the negative and not be victimized by giving it power. Obviously renunciation is closely aligned to the power of judgement at this level. The wonderful result is that by choosing to refuse entry into your consciousness, negative entities have no choice but to die. It is always important to remember that negative conditions have no choice, but you do. By choosing to avoid gossiping, resentment, or fear, you keep the high watch for your consciousness. It is your responsibility not to allow another's negative mental suggestion to infiltrate your mind and heart. In this way renunciation is a preventative. If practiced enough, it can be developed into a permanent attitude of "NO" toward all that is untrue and negative.

Your greatest opportunities for growth and your greatest challenges will come to you through other people. So it is paramount to remember that renunciation is your ability to forgive and release others.

You might say it is easier said than done. Remember the true definition of forgiveness. You must reverse the situation by giving for. Give love for hurt. Give tolerance for impatience. Give strength for weakness. It is up to you to give for and to give forth to God's qualities. The instant you give love instead of reacting with anger, you are free of all negative patterns. This fress you of resentment which might have enslaved you. You must renounce any negative relationship with others so that you may respond rather than react. Loving response allows you to free others from your consciousness as a negative experience. When you release others, you release yourself. That which you have been condemning in others has, in reality, been self-condemnation. It is a common expression that one forgives but doesn't forget. In this case the release is not complete. You must forget the past and let bygones be bygones. Any harboring of resentment chains you to the entire limiting experience.

One must always be willing to forgive himself as well as others. Self-condemnation is destructive and prevents consciousness development. It is necessary to be specific in calling upon your gift of renunciation. Actually put the words and ideas through your mind, and tell yourself that you forgive yourself and that you approve of yourself. After all, if you don't approve of yourself, who can? Here is a recommendation. Using your own name say, "John Smith, I love you; I bless you; and I have faith in you". Take your time and be gentle but firm. You will experience the greatest release of your life as the divine gift of renunciation is activated in your soul. Tremendous spiritual power is released to act on your behalf upon your invitation. Do not neglect yourself in spiritual matters. Speak the word of truth for yourself.

Renunciation creates a vacuum. You are making more room for spiritual awareness as you eliminate broken-down opinions and false beliefs about yourself. Denial is a form of renunciation. A denial is a statement about something in your consciousness that you want to be rid of. If you are experiencing jealousy, make a statement that there is no room or need for jealousy in your consciousness. Then be still. A vacuum is created and your soul is but waiting to be fulfilled. It is important, therefore, that you have an affirmation about the truth of your being. For instance, "I am light and love and filled with the power of God". If you do not have an affirmation, you will eventually drift back into the jealous pattern. You cannot build upon erroneous beliefs, so you have to eliminate them and replace them with truth.

Renunciation is entirely an inner process. Do not try to deny away disease, personalities, and outer conditions. Denials are actually used on your own beliefs and attitudes not on outer things. You are adjusting your consciousness to the good rather than trying to rearrange the world. Once you have come to understand this, you will make great strides in personal transformation. Your true self is the Christ-self. Denials separate negative emotions from your true self in understanding. When you come to understand that your true self is not sick, angry, hurt, or poor, then you have renounced all these qualities from your consciousness and cannot experience them in life.

SCRIPTURE

"And he said to them all, if any man will come after me, let him deny himself." (Lu. 12:9)

"Let the wicked forsake his way." (Is. 55:7)

"I will lay down my life for thy sake." (Jn. 13:37)

"We . . . have renounced the hidden things of dishonesty"-(2 Co. 4:1,2)

"Love not the world, neither the things that are in the world." (1 Jn. 2:15)

QUESTIONS

1. What are the two main functions of renunciation?
2. Should the intent be to remove outer things?
3. How do you give power to outer things?
4. How do you eliminate a negative belief?
5. What brings things into existence and vice versa?
6. Are overwhelming conditions and turmoil a bad sign?
7. What spiritual gift is closely related to renunciation in avoiding negativity?
8. Where will you find your greatest opportunities for growth?
9. How does one forgive?
10. Who must you forgive?
11. What is meant by creating a vacuum?
12. Where does renunciation take place?

DENIAL

Nothing unwanted needs to remain in my consciousness and life experience.

AFFIRMATION

I am now filled with wholeness, light, and a sense of well-being.

LIFE

LIFE   *is my ability to mend, restore, and draw upon the living Christ for all life functions.*

LIFE   *is my progress, attainment, and mastery.*

PREVIEW

1. LIFE is realized at three levels: subconsciousness, consciousness, and superconsciousness.

2. LIFE is the ability to heal and restore.

3. There is no such thing as death.

4. Making love is a spiritual experience.

5. LIFE is your progress, attainment, and mastery.

If you were to ask a fish to point the way to water, he wouldn't know which way to point. It is very much the same for human beings when trying to consider life. One might answer when questioned about life, "I am life, I do it, I live it". It is taken so much for granted that it is seldom recognized as a God-given gift which serves in special ways in consciousness development.

Awareness is the key. Mankind is the only entity on earth that is aware of self or can think in abstracts. Therefore the destiny of the earth is in the hands of mankind, or, to be more specific, in the consciousness of mankind. So the greatest thing an individual can do is to dedicate himself to the development of awareness. In developing your awareness of your spiritual gifts, you are growing into the understanding that you are more than a quantity--you are the absolute. You are more than strong--you are strength itself. You are more than wise--you are wisdom itself. You are more than loving and orderly--you are love and order. And above all, you are not merely living--you are life. Sometimes it is easy to slip into the belief that you are developing one of these gifts. That is impossible because they are all perfect in you now. You are perfect, and the only thing you can develop is your awareness of your perfection. You can't develop faith in you, for it is perfect in you. However, you do want to develop your awareness and conscious use of that perfect faith. This holds true for all of your twelve wonderful gifts.

So it is with life. You express life at three levels of awareness: subconscious, conscious, and superconscious. Actually, it is expressed when you are unconscious as well, but we are primarily interested in the first three levels. Life is expressed through you constantly in ways that you don't have to think about. Your organs function automatically. Your tissues and cells mend and grow without your thinking of them, and your various systems operate and coordinate all on their own. Even your emotions and beliefs alter and protect you without your conscious awareness. Divine Life pours through you as a channel of God at these unconscious and subconscious levels. But even though life is fully operative at these levels, they are not the levels where you may exercise choice. It is at the conscious level where you do your choice making. This is the level where you direct your thoughts and feelings.

The superconscious, of course, is God in you. You already know all that is. You might not be aware that you already have the answers, but they are there nevertheless. It is when you turn to the superconscious from the conscious level, that miracles begin to happen.

Life is the ability to heal and restore. When you, at the conscious level, call upon the Christ in you to direct healing energy and light to restore your body to perfection, you are placing your body into complete charge of your Christ-self. God in you is your Christ-self, and it is at this level of superconsciousness that healing takes place. You of yourself do nothing other than make a spiritual choice. The illness makes no choice; the body makes no choice; and the Christ in you makes no choice. Only you at a conscious level of self-awareness can make choices in directing the flow of Spirit. By stilling yourself to Divine Life you activate the living spirit, or superconscious, in you to do that which is needed. If illness manifests, it is a sign that something is out of order in the subconscious level. The subconscious always produces a body according to its own nature. Order can be restored in the body by consciously directing and beholding the perfection that is already there.

There is no such thing as death. The real you is not alive. The real you is life itself. Being alive is merely a term that we associate with life as it is expressed through your present body. We have erroneously come to the conclusion that the opposite of being alive is being dead. It is a logical conclusion when one is unaware that he is the life itself. If one is to judge by outer appearances, you are either dead or alive. It is really a matter where you have no choice. You are life just as you are faith, wisdom, order, strength, judgement, love, power, imagination, understanding, will, zeal, and renunciation. You do, however, have the choice of entering the third dimension as being alive. It is that state where you are consciously aware of being alive. Moving on into another dimension is a frightening idea if you don't understand that life in you continues. This results in the fear and belief that your very being can be extinguished. It is a belief in death. Isn't it wonderful to overcome the idea of death? It is the first step in eliminating the aging process.

Not only are we coming into the awareness that there is no death, but we are beginning to understand that birth is much more than the choosing of a new body. Birth is being born again into higher awareness. In the process of soul development, you are born countless times. Sometimes you enter a new body upon a new birth, but not always. Every time you receive new insight and inspiration to where it alters your consciousness, you are born again. You are a new you, not subject to previous limitation.

New birth is always a decision of the soul. Perhaps parents think they decided to have another child, but in reality it is the soul that is choosing a new set of earthly parents. Actually the subject of procreation, love-making, and new birth should be clarified. All three are spiritual experiences not to be confused with evil, sin, and morality. It has been thought in the past that a man and woman should join as one in sexual intercourse for one purpose only, that of having children. This belief is based on fear and ignorance and should be discarded along with all guilt-control devices. The life process includes procreation, healing, regeneration, and also the marvelous exchange which takes place in love-making. Too much emphasis has been given to the dangers of getting caught up in lust and sexual pro. miscuity. More emphasis should be placed on the presence of God within. If a person truly understands his spirituality, he needn't overcompensate in any area. In reality, making love is a spiritual experience, and it is a means of sharing life. It is when a person is ignorant of his Christ-self that he considers it an activity which is merely to satisfy his own ego and sexual drive. If you think you are out of balance in this area, don't fight sense appetite. Rather enfold yourself and your loved one in spiritual light and sense appetite will be transformed into spiritual fulfillment.

Life is progress, attainment, and mastery. As life flows through you, you will feel you need to progress. You cannot stay at one level and remain content for any length of time. The Christ in you is ever urging you to attain your next level of consciousness. But in truth, mastering your present level isn't as great a challenge as becoming willing to move on to the next. There is one way you can identify when it is time to move on. A challenge or opportunity will present itself to you, and it will appear to be greater than what you can handle. It will demand that you rely upon Spirit for the resolution.

It is not the challenge or opportunity that makes you grow. It is your willingness to rely on Spirit, to act as a willing channel, that lifts you from one level of consciousness to another. You have drawn the event into your life for your progress, attainment, and mastery. So when you see a wonderful new challenge, just realize that it is time to move on to new ways and insights. Rather than resisting challenges, allow God to do his transforming work in and through you. You are being polished as a bright light that others may see by. When faced with great change, still yourself to Divine Life and you will be transformed.

SCRIPTURES

"Choose life, that both thou and thy seed may live."
(De. 30:19)
"To be spiritually minded is life and peace." (Ro. 8:6)
"He that hath not the son of God hath not life." (1 Jn. 5:12)
"Man doth not live by bread only, but by every word
that proceedeth out of the mouth of the Lord doth men
live." (De. 8:3)
"God is not the God of the dead, but of the living." (Mat.
22:32)

QUESTIONS

1. Is self-awareness important to spiritual development?
2. Can you develop your spiritual gifts?
3. What are the three levels of expression of life?
4. Can one level affect another?
5. What is meant by "being alive"?
6. When is one dead?
7. Who makes the decision as to when you are born?
8. Can you be born more than once during one lifetime?
9. Should one reduce love-making to be more spiritual?
10. What causes uncontrollable lust?
11. Why do challenges appear just when everything seems to be doing fine?
12. Does a challenge make you grow?

DENIAL

There is no such thing as an absence of life.

AFFIRMATION

Divine Life fills me now, healing, restoring, making me whole and well.

ABOUT THE AUTHOR

William A. Warch was the founding minister of the
Church of Christian Living in Anaheim, California. He was a
member of the executive board of the International New
Thought Alliance and actively involved in their youth program.
He was the host minister for the nationally known, "Inner
Space Odyssey" Seminars which were designed to present the
greatest people of New Thought enlightenment to the public.
Reverend Warch drew upon a wide variety of New Thought
teachings in presenting his works.